Butterflies and leaves.

Japanese
Silk Designs
in Full Color

Edited by
M. P. VERNEUIL

DOVER PUBLICATIONS, INC.
Mineola, New York

Publisher's Note

During the latter half of the nineteenth century, after treaties had opened up international commerce with Japan, the art and objects of that country became widely popular. For the first time, European artists were exposed to Japanese woodblock prints and silk designs and their fascination with these styles greatly influenced the development of the Art Nouveau movement in France.

The present volume reproduces, in full color, a selection of sixty plates from M. P. Verneuil's original portfolio *Étoffes Japonaises, Tissées & Brochées*, first published by the Librairie Centrale des Beaux-Arts in Paris in 1910. An influential teacher of Art Nouveau decoration, artist M[aurice] P[illard] Verneuil (1869–1942) had already made outstanding contributions to the use of design motifs based on plant and animal life. Inspired by the flood of Japanese art to Europe at that time, Verneuil culled a portfolio of stunning examples of authentic Japanese woven and printed fabrics. Taken as a whole, the designs showcased in this book, most of which are based on elegant organic forms, combine the flowing, curvilinear style that became the hallmark of Art Nouveau with an imaginative use of stylized Japanese art.

Bibliographical Note

This Dover edition, first published in 2004, is a selection of sixty plates from *Étoffes Japonaises, Tissées & Brochées*, originally published by the Librairie Centrale des Beaux-Arts, Paris, in 1910.

DOVER *Pictorial Archive* SERIES

Library of Congress Cataloging-in-Publication Data

Etoffes japonaises, tissées & brochées. English. Selections.
   Japanese silk designs in full color / edited by M.P. Verneuil.
      p. cm. — (Dover pictorial archive series)
   Originally published: Paris : Librairie centrale des beaux-arts, 1910.
   ISBN 0-486-43717-5 (pbk.)
   1. Textile design — Japan — Themes, motives. 2. Brocade — Japan — Themes, motives. I. Verneuil, M. P. (Maurice Pillard), 1869–   II. Title. III. Series.
NK8984.A1E76213 2004
746'.0952—dc22
                                                                        2004051979

Manufactured in the United States of America
Dover Publications, Inc., 31 East 2nd Street, Mineola, N.Y. 11501

Butterflies and chrysanthemums.

Ornamental motifs.

LEFT: Hydrangeas. RIGHT: Palm trees.

LEFT, TOP: Animals and decorative flowers. LEFT, BOTTOM: Birds and trees.
RIGHT: Birds and flowers in cherry trees.

LEFT: Decorative motifs. RIGHT: Peacocks and peonies.

TOP: Stylized flowers. BOTTOM: Waves.

Peacocks.

LEFT AND RIGHT: Cranes.

8

Glycines on trelliswork.

TOP: Birds and peonies. BOTTOM: Flying birds and stylized plants.

LEFT: Chrysanthemums. RIGHT: Peonies.

LEFT: Stylized figures. RIGHT, TOP: Bird with checkerwork design. RIGHT, BOTTOM: Children playing.

Laburnums on trelliswork.

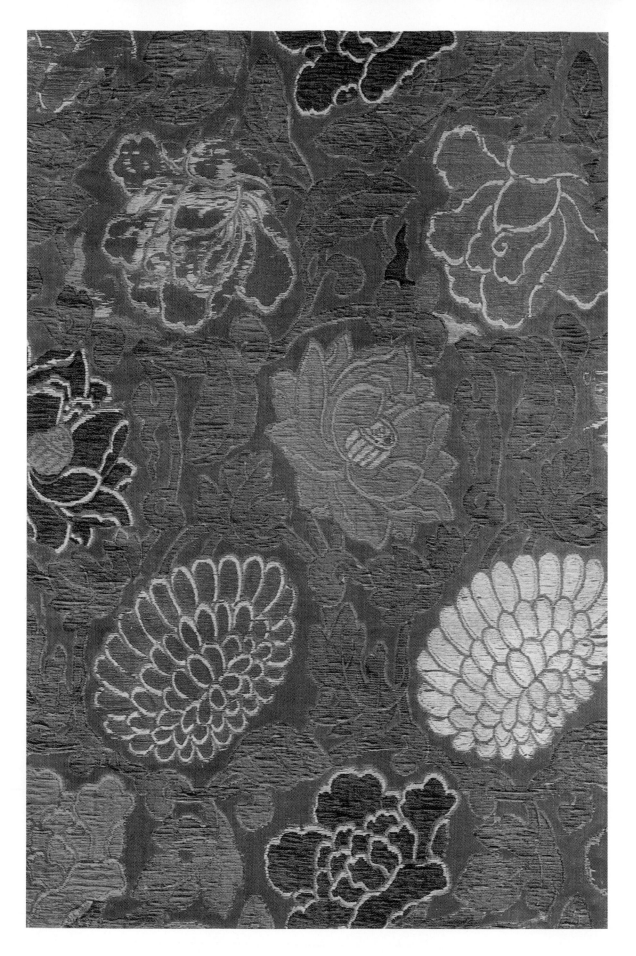

Chrysanthemums, lotus, and peonies.

LEFT AND RIGHT: Flying cranes.

15

LEFT: Peonies. RIGHT: Stylized flowers.

Flowers and marrow leaves.

TOP, LEFT: Shells on a geometric background. TOP, RIGHT: Flying cranes and chrysanthemums. BOTTOM: Sunflowers.

Waves and stylized sailing vessel.

Birds and stylized flowers.

TOP, LEFT: Fern leaves. TOP, RIGHT: Figures. BOTTOM: Night scenes.

Decorative flowers.

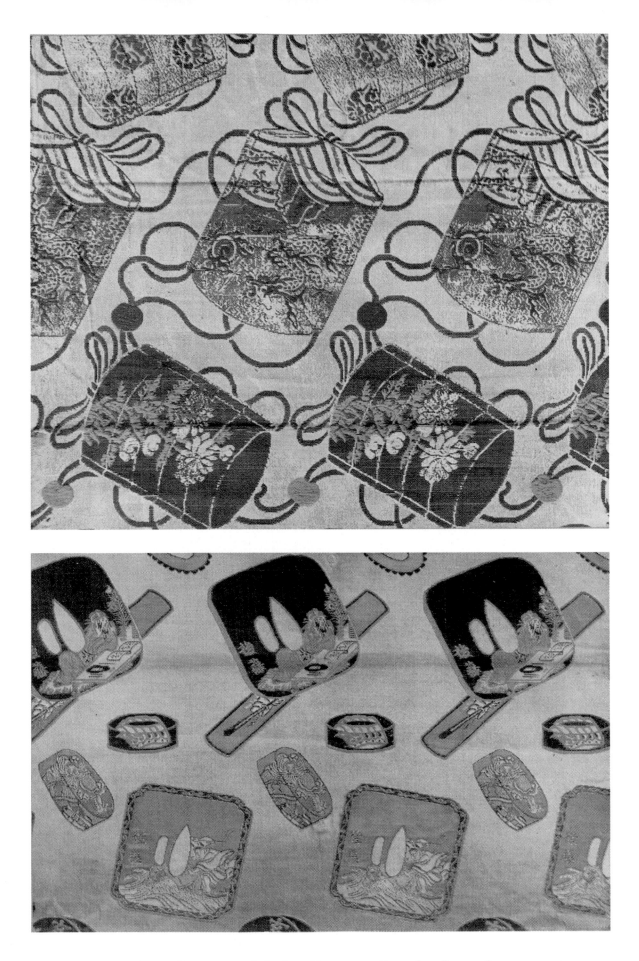

Top: Ornamental design. Bottom: Guards of swords.

Stylized cranes with geometrical designs.

Dragonflies.

LEFT: Ornamental motifs. RIGHT: Flowers and stylized animals.

Birds and camellias.

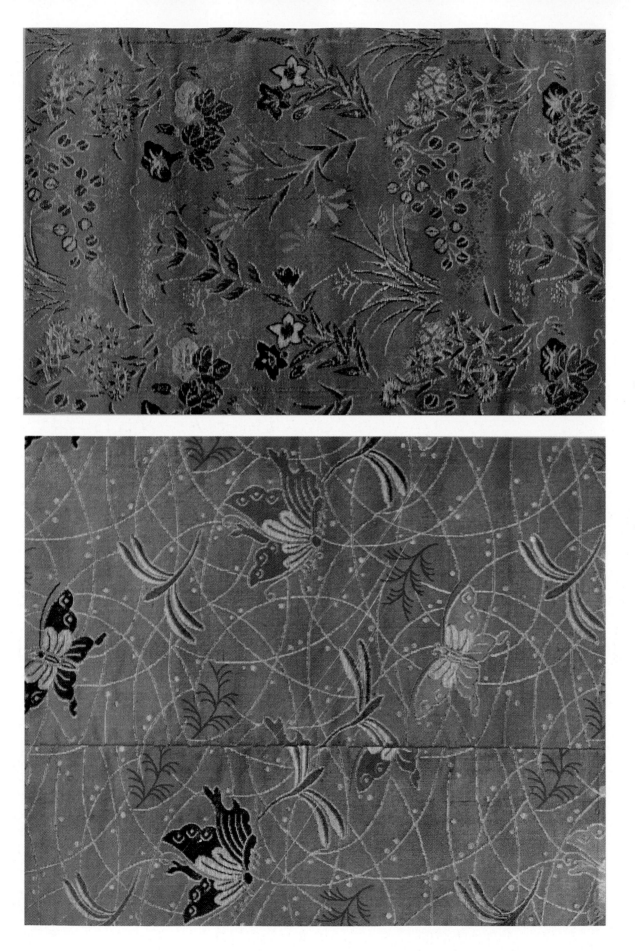

LEFT: Butterflies. RIGHT: Various flowers.

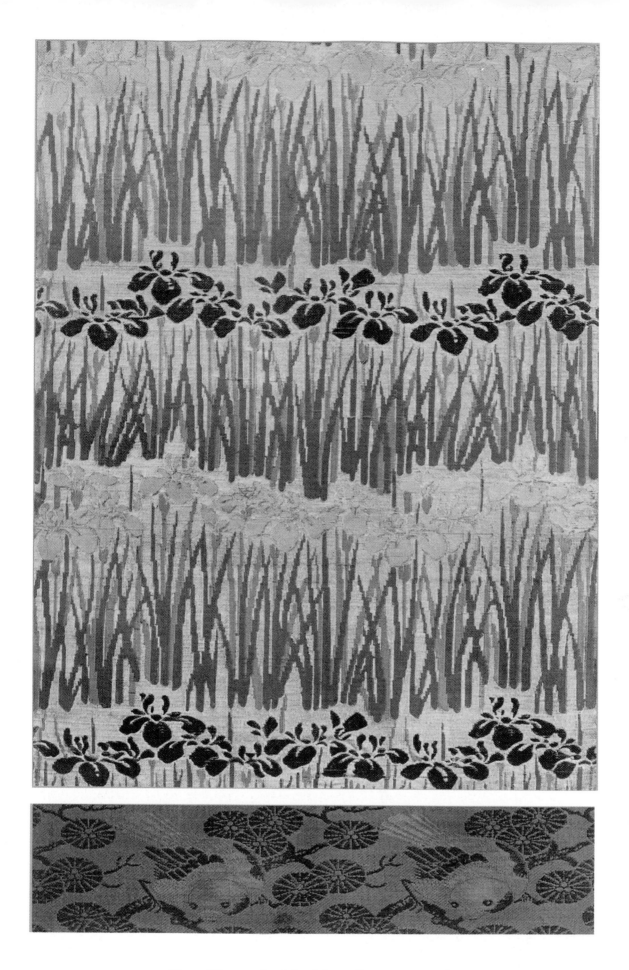

TOP: Blue and white irises. BOTTOM: Birds.

LEFT AND RIGHT: Butterflies.

Flowers on a geometric background.

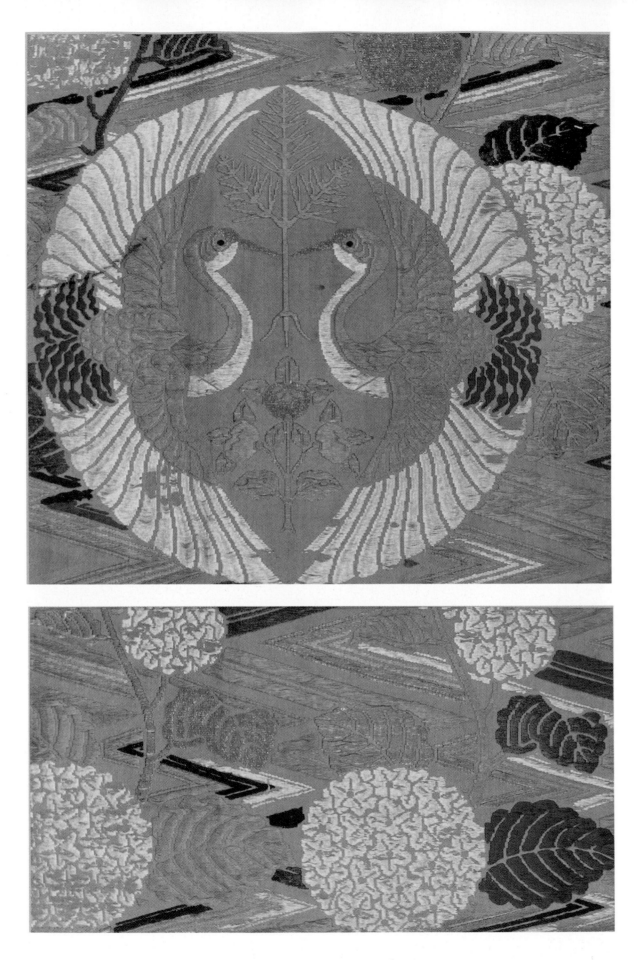

TOP: Cranes. BOTTOM: Hydrangea.

Flowers and leaves.

LEFT: Birds in flight. RIGHT, TOP: Ornamental design. RIGHT, BOTTOM: Dragon and foliage.

34

Peonies.

Birds and bamboo.

TOP: Birds and stylized plants. BOTTOM: Flowers and butterflies.

Stylized figures.

Flying geese above the tide.

TOP, LEFT: Geometric motifs. TOP, RIGHT: Ornamental motifs.
BOTTOM: Ornamental motifs.

Cranes and clouds.

TOP: Dragons and peonies. BOTTOM: Flying birds and foliage.

Peonies.

Butterflies and foliage.

Stylized flowers.

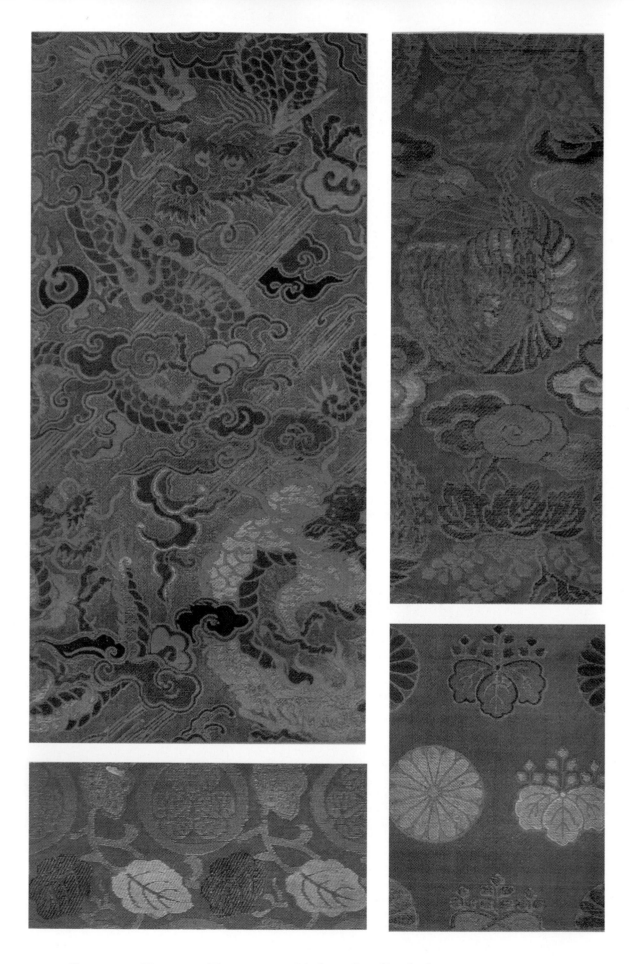

Top, left: Dragons. Top, right: Birds and stylized plants. Bottom, left:
Leaves and rosettes. Bottom, right: Paulownia and rosettes.

Peonies.

TOP AND BOTTOM: Stylized flowers.

Ornamental motifs.

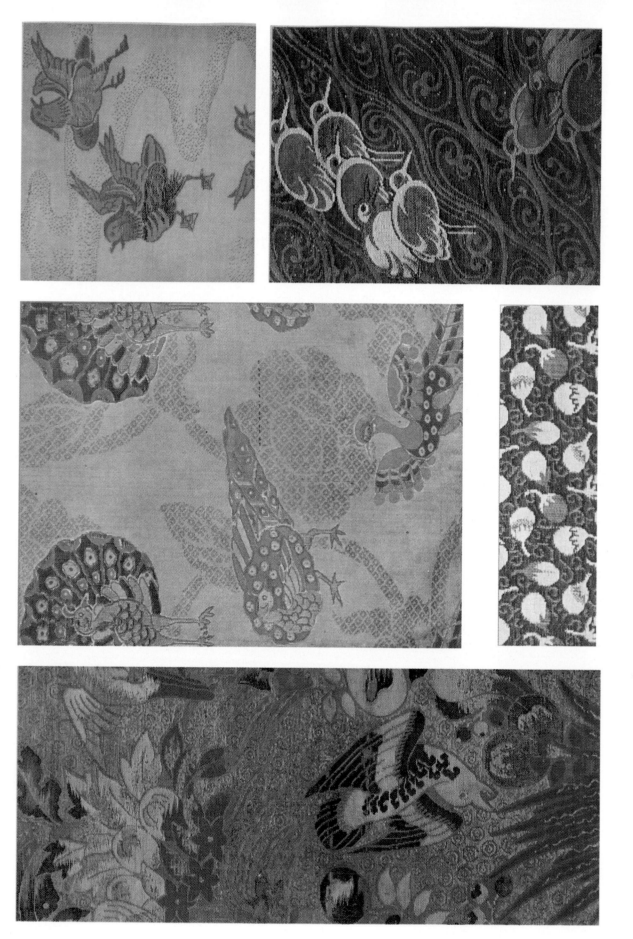

LEFT: Plants and birds. MIDDLE, TOP: Stylized peacocks. MIDDLE, BOTTOM: Fruits. RIGHT, TOP: Birds. RIGHT, BOTTOM: Stylized cranes.

Stylized flowers.

TOP, LEFT: Flowers and birds. TOP, RIGHT: Stylized flowers.
MIDDLE, RIGHT: Chrysanthemums. BOTTOM: Floral motifs.

Dragons and flowers in a geometric background.

TOP, LEFT: Stylized flowers. TOP, RIGHT: Tiger and tortoise design.
BOTTOM: Ornamental motifs.

54

Ornamental motifs.

LEFT, TOP: Foliage. LEFT, BOTTOM: Flowers and leaves. RIGHT: Passion flower.

56

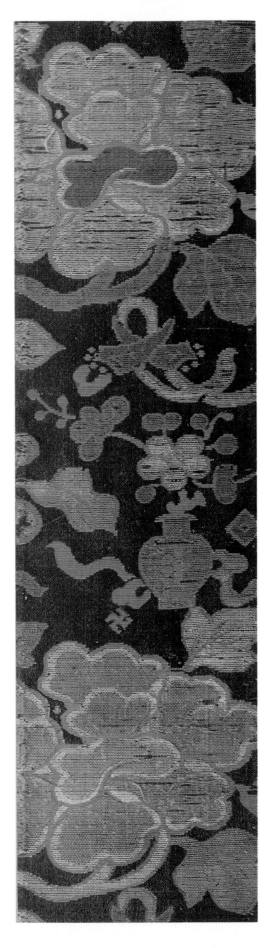

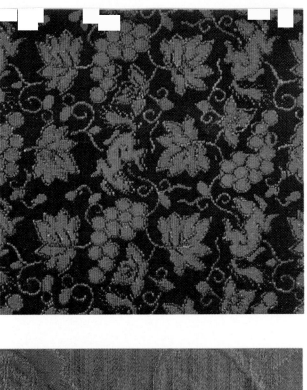

LEFT: Flowers and ornamental motifs. RIGHT, TOP: Foxes and grapes.
RIGHT, BOTTOM: Ornamental motifs.

Ornamental motif.

LEFT, TOP: Foliage. LEFT, BOTTOM: Paulownia. MIDDLE: Paulownia on a geometric background. RIGHT, TOP: Marrow leaves and geometric design. RIGHT, BOTTOM: Leaves and fruit on a striped background.